Donna Spencer

FACILITATING DESIGN THINKING WORKSHOPS

A practical guide for new and experienced facilitators

Publisher: Donna Spencer

https://maadmob.com.au

TABLE OF CONTENTS

3   *Introduction*

5   CHAPTER 1
     What is a Design Thinking Workshop

12   CHAPTER 2
     Planning a Design Thinking Workshop

28   CHAPTER 3
     Running a Design Thinking Workshop

47   CHAPTER 4
     Managing People

56   CHAPTER 5
     Online Workshops

59   *Conclusion*

61   *Resources*

63   *Index*

64   *About the Author*

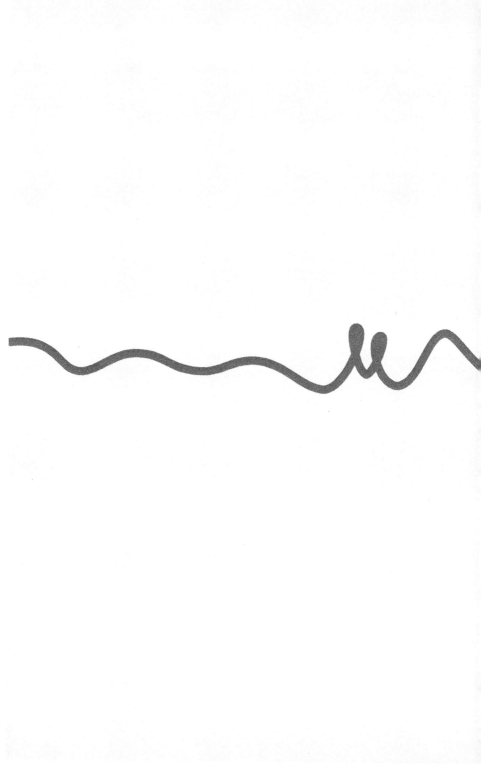

Have you ever found yourself in a workshop where you were trying to figure out the next product feature, solve a complex problem or make collective decisions? How did it go? Did you feel energized, able to contribute, that your contribution was valuable, and the workshop was a good use of your time? Or did you feel uncertain about why you were there, that you weren't being listened to and nothing would happen at the end? I've certainly found myself more in the second kind than the first. But when I have been in the first kind, it has been a fabulous and rewarding experience!

Are you now being asked to run this kind of workshop and want to make it more like the former than the latter? Then this book is for you.

I really like writing books on very practical topics (this is my fifth!), and to me one of the best ways to be practical is to focus on a very specific topic. In this case, this meant not writing a general book on 'facilitation' or 'running workshops' but specifically on 'facilitating design thinking workshops'. A nice, narrow focus helped me to write a concise, practical book that you can read in a short sitting and use right away.

If you've picked it up (or I've given it to you) and you aren't running exactly this kind of workshop, there is still a ton of useful advice and tips that will help with facilitating any kind of group activity, including meetings and training.

ABOUT ME

I've been standing on my feet in front of groups since I was promoted to the role of 'crew trainer' of a large fast-food chain at 15. Even early in my non-restaurant career, I figured out that I was always going to be the one who took the lead in a group and helped people work together.

I've taught hundreds of educational workshops, to tiny and huge audiences. I've facilitated hundreds of regular meetings. And I've facilitated loads of design thinking workshops and design hackathons. Hopefully most of them were good ones!

I'm also a practicing digital designer with a focus on complex, novel software. I'm a player and game master of role-playing games, which involves remarkably similar facilitation skills to those I describe in this book. And when not doing those things, I'm weaving, sewing or reading crime novels.

FACILITATING...

The success of a design thinking workshop comes directly from it's planning, structure and facilitation. A workshop isn't about putting people together and just hoping they'll work it out. A great workshop involves a deliberate plan for how a group gets from the start to the end, in a way that still lets them feel in control of the process. It's a surprisingly tough thing to do, needing structure, flexibility, time management and people management—all while you're on your feet in front of a room full of people. It's as rewarding as it is difficult!

DESIGN THINKING...

Design thinking is a popular approach used to come up with solutions for all kinds of problems. It is highly collaborative, super creative and can achieve great outcomes.

One of the core ideas in design thinking is to identify a large number of potential solutions before deciding on a direction—not just taking a particular solution as the only way. I've been involved in design thinking activities for topics such as:

- Detailed design for a new product feature
- Planning future product features
- Exploring how to improve productivity in a small construction company, without getting rid of jobs

- Solving the recycling crisis
- The future of TV
- How might technology be used to improve the customer experience at a large football stadium
- How to use a physical space to improve educational outcomes for students

WORKSHOPS

Design thinking is always about people working together to explore the problem and discuss solutions. As such, a lot of it is executed in the form of workshops—getting people in a room (physical or online) to work together for a defined amount of time with specific outcomes in mind.

In a great workshop everyone can contribute their expertise, feels heard and included, is heard and included, and a concrete plan is made with next steps. Everyone feels like the workshop was a good use of their time.

A poor workshop is exactly the opposite. People feel like the time was a waste and that they could have been doing something else more useful. Their expertise isn't valued. And they won't want to repeat the experience.

Continue reading to learn how to plan, structure and facilitate great workshops!

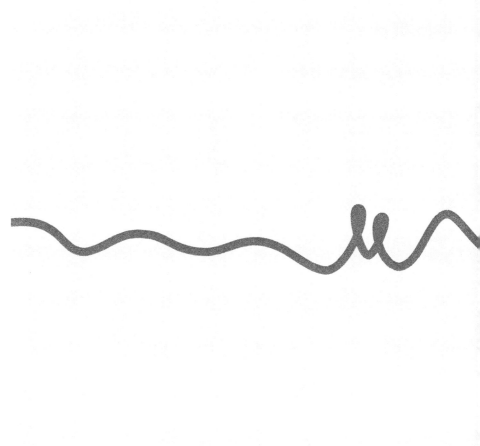

A design thinking workshop pulls together a diverse group of people to solve a problem in a collaborative way.

Design thinking workshops are particularly good for problems that don't have clear and obvious solutions, and where you want to explore a range of different approaches. As I said in the introduction, I've been in workshops about the future of TV, how to better use physical spaces, how to apply new technologies to existing situations, and how to solve very complex issues such as waste. These were all topics where there wasn't a single, obvious solution.

Design thinking workshops should not be full of designers. In fact, the majority of participants will usually be people who wouldn't normally be actively involved in designing new products or services, such as subject matter experts, business stakeholders and users. Everyone contributes, not just designers and technologists.

Design thinking workshops aren't just long meetings where people present and listen. They have a clear set of desired outcomes and are structured so most the time is spent actively working as a group to achieve those outcomes. They are usually time-constrained with the intent of achieving a lot in a short time.

WHAT HAPPENS IN A WORKSHOP?

Design thinking workshops can be as short as half a day or as long as a week. Despite the differences in length, they follow a fairly similar pattern. My general approach looks like this:

- Introduce the workshop
- Warm up the group
- Understand the current context
- Generate ideas
- Select ideas to explore in more detail
- Describe ideas in more detail
- Prioritize and plan next steps

Here's that list in a diagram, where the vertical axis is both the volume of ideas and the energy of the group, and the horizontal axis is time.

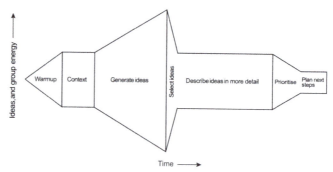

Figure 1: The flow of ideas and energy over time

Let's look at what happens in each of those sections.

Warmup

The warmup part of the workshop does two very important things. It gets people ready to work together, and it starts introducing skills that people will need in other places in the workshop. It's so important that I have an entire section about warmups in chapter 3.

Context

After a warmup, I always take time to discuss what's happening now, what brought us together for a workshop, and start to get everyone on the same page. The idea is for the group to all have at least a similar understanding when they go into the middle of the workshop.

The actual content of this section varies depending on what the workshop is about. You might discuss and demonstrate the user needs you're addressing; you might discuss changes in the external environment that are affecting the business; you might explain new technologies before exploring how they can be used.

Idea generation

With a good understanding of the current situation and why we're here, we're ready to go into the idea-generation part of the workshop.

This is the part that design thinking workshops are really known for—where the group works together to come up ideas. This isn't the time for thinking deeply, critiquing or considering viability—it's the time to create loads of ideas, and hopefully ideas that haven't been tried before.

This part of the workshop is usually time constrained. I usually do two rounds in this section. The first round gets initial ideas out. The second round builds on those ideas— usually going crazier and more unexpected.

As with warmups, this is super-important and there are more details in the Brainstorming and idea generation part of chapter 3.

Idea description and definition

Next, we take the ideas the group came up with, choose some (usually by voting or combining ideas) and work them through in more detail. Where the first step was about coming up with unbounded ideas, this second step is about understanding how they really might work.

I give this section plenty of time. People need to really get into the idea and think it through. In a short workshop, I run this section across a break to give people even more time for reflective thinking.

Prioritisation and next steps

Design thinking workshops aim to identify practical ways of solving a problem. That means they don't end when the ideas are created.

When I plan a workshop, a lot of my clients want to skip this step and make decisions themselves later. I so strongly discourage this that I won't agree to facilitate a workshop unless the workshop participants are involved in the decisions about next steps—after participating and giving their energy, they do need to see their input taken seriously.

A REAL EXAMPLE

My client ran a business that manufactured cardboard and cardboard boxes. They wanted to use technology to reduce waste, improve productivity and safety, and still protect jobs.

Given there were many ways to approach this kind of problem, and many potential solutions, we decided to run a design thinking workshop. We could use the expertise across the company, and genuinely involve the whole team in the process. My client had never done anything like this before and was understandably nervous about the whole thing. But they were willing to give it a go as the time commitment was fairly low and the activity low-risk.

We invited factory managers, machine operators and sales staff. None of them had ever been involved in an activity like this either. They'd rarely been involved in anything to do with their work processes and were a bit cynical about whether the workshop was just a way of pretending to listen to them.

In the workshop itself, we started by creating a context map, describing what 'now' looked like and what was influencing a need for change (in the workshop structure diagram, this covered the warmup, introduction and context sections). We had a short presentation on possible technologies and what they did.

For our idea-generation section, first everyone described an ideal future, focusing on it from their own perspective and expertise. We then brainstormed to create ideas based on what seemed like whacky combinations of problems and technologies. The group shared their ideas with each other; and with some careful facilitation I encouraged them to create what seemed like crazier ideas.

Everyone presented (without any critique at this point) and we talked about the viability of some of the ideas. The group voted on the ones to continue in the workshop.

After a break, smaller groups wove the ideas into day-in-the-life stories, so they could really consider how the idea would be used in the factory, its consequences, and what would be needed to achieve such a change. Again, the groups presented back.

To prioritize follow-up work, we plotted the ideas on a grid according to how much they'd contribute to waste reduction and productivity, against a timeline of now, soon, or much later.

The whole group agreed on a plan to get started (by this point, I was hardly facilitating—they were doing it themselves) and went away with a solid plan to start some changes.

It was a successful workshop, everyone was involved, and they went away with some great ideas to follow up. All in less than a day!

CHAPTER SUMMARY

A design thinking workshop brings together a diverse group of people (primarily experts and users, not designers and technologists) to generate a range of solutions to a problem, to describe those solutions in some detail, and make a solid plan for next steps.

While every workshop will be completely different in length, topics and activities, they do follow a fairly standard approach which involves getting everyone on the same page, generating ideas, choosing some to go into more detail, prioritizing, and planning next steps.

Read on to learn how to plan a workshop.

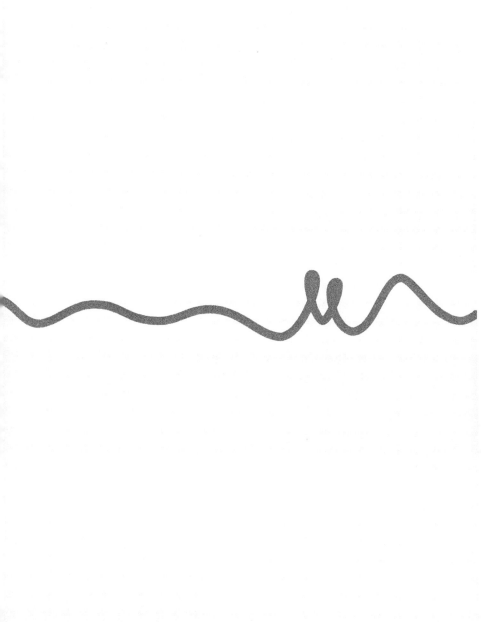

A successful design thinking workshop relies on two things—great planning and great in-the-moment facilitation. As these two are highly connected, they really should be done by the same person.

FACILITATING WITHOUT CONTRIBUTING

Before we even start discussing planning, we should discuss the facilitator's role in the workshop.

The role of a facilitator in a design thinking workshop is just that—to facilitate the workshop. To help the group get from the beginning to the end, with everyone contributing.

The facilitator's role is to not add to the substance of the workshop at all. When a facilitator adds ideas to a workshop, participants feel pushed towards their opinion and many will stop contributing or lose trust in the activity.

If you are planning to facilitate for a team or topic you know, you must be able to stand back from the topic and just facilitate. This can be especially difficult if you are a designer on a project and are used to doing the problem-solving and designing steps!

If you would like to add your ideas to a workshop, find someone else to facilitate it.

WORKSHOP GOALS

The first step of planning any design thinking workshop is to have an exceptionally clear idea of its goals and outcomes.

This will usually involve one or more discussions with the person who has asked you to arrange the workshop (I'm just going to use the word 'client' from now—even if you will be working with a colleague, they're your client when you are a facilitator).

If your client hasn't been involved in a design thinking workshop before, they may not know what it can achieve and what it might look like. They may be asking as they've heard a workshop is a good idea. So, part of your initial discussions might be just talking about their general expectations.

To figure out the goals and desired outcomes you can ask questions like:

- What was the trigger for considering a workshop? Who came up with the idea?
- What do you want to achieve with this workshop? (Yep, that's an obvious one)
- Do you want to explore opportunities, get an agreement between the group members, or generate more detailed design ideas?
- What do you imagine will happen during the workshop? (although this isn't a 'goal' question, it's a good one for uncovering expectations)
- What should we all have achieved when we leave the room?
- How will you use the outcomes from the workshop?
- How does this workshop fit into other work that is happening?
- How do you want people to feel during and after the workshop?
- What would you hope people say about the workshop?

These kinds of questions should give you a very good idea of what the what the client wants to get out of the workshop.

You'll also want to ask a lot of questions that will start you thinking about the detailed planning of the workshop, its length and what you might do during it:

- Who do you expect to attend?
- How will users / customers be involved?
- How will subject matter experts be involved?

- Will people be able to attend, and stay for the full time? (I'll cover this later, but they do need to be able to attend the whole thing)
- Have you, or the participants been involved in a design thinking workshop before? How did it go? (it's especially important to know if people have never been involved in a workshop; or if they been involved in workshops that didn't produce anything)
- What 'elephants in the room', emotional landmines or people issues should we anticipate? (there will always be some)
- What will you do if the session goes in a direction that's unexpected? Will you accept the outcomes?
- Will the group be able to make decisions during the workshop? Will they have enough information? Are they empowered to make decisions?
- What do you need for the outputs of the workshop? Do you need photographs, recordings of the ideas or a full report?
- Can a design thinking workshop achieve the goals?

With a good understanding of the goals, consider whether a design thinking workshop is a good way to achieve them.

Design thinking workshops are great for:
- Getting people to work together effectively
- Getting a shared understanding of the problem to be solved
- Generating many new ideas for a problem
- Generating practical ideas for understandable topics
- Getting a lot done in a small amount of time
- Getting a group to collectively decide on next steps

Design thinking workshop aren't suitable for:
- Solving very complex problems in a constrained time frame: Complex problems have too many moving parts to solve in a workshop and attempts to do so just come

up with shallow solutions.
- Coming up with detailed solutions for anything other than simple problems: There's usually just not enough time to work through anything complex.
- Solving problems that are difficult to understand: A group can't come up with great ideas if they can't understand the problem.

There are other situations where you'll be asked to facilitate, and it doesn't feel like a design thinking workshop is a good fit. Here are some other warning bells:

- There is no plan for following up the outcomes.
- It feels like a token effort to get people to talk to each other.
- There is no representation from subject matter experts or users.
- If users aren't involved (and there are times when they won't be) there is also no user research—everything will be based on participants' opinions.
- It feels like a 'rubber stamp' to something that has already been decided.
- Attendees are too busy to stay for the whole workshop and expect that they can drop in and out.
- The client expects a magic outcome in a short amount of time.

There's really no point running workshops that can't achieve their goals—they are a waste of time for participants, and they'll be hesitant to get involved next time. I call these 'design theatre'—they're high energy, fun, look good in photos, but ultimately don't achieve anything and instead hurt the practice of design thinking and collaborative work, your reputation as a facilitator and your client's reputation for collaborating.

If you're being asked to run a workshop that sounds like it can't work, push back (or decline if you're in a position to). Encourage your client to do some traditional research and analysis work to learn about the problem, then discuss how to 'bite off' some parts of it that a design thinking workshop may be able to address.

Doing a dry run

If you, the client and the participants have never been involved in a design thinking activity before, and the topic has important consequences, consider running a lower-risk workshop before the main workshop—to get everyone familiar with the feel and the process.

PROBLEM STATEMENTS

One way to describe the purpose of the workshop is a problem statement or a challenge statement. This describes the topic and the goal of the workshop in a simple way.

Problem statements keep the workshop focused. Without a focus, participants won't have a clear idea of what they are working towards, and will easily go on tangents.

Problem statements can come from all kinds of places. Sometimes your client will have a clear idea of the problem to be solved and will be able to describe it clearly. Sometimes it will be the outcome from customer research. Sometimes the client will know that there is something to be solved but hasn't quite figured it out yet.

In some cases, I've run a workshop to decide on the problem to be addressed—it sounds strange to have a workshop to plan the workshop, but I knew that if we went in with a vague problem, it would waste everyone's time.

Problem statements are often phrased as 'how might we…' questions (though if this format doesn't work for your statement, don't feel that you must use it). 'How might we' is a useful structure as it communicates that the problem doesn't yet have a solution, and 'we' are going to work on it together.

Good problem statements:
- Describe problems, not solutions
- Are open, and imply that there is a solution
- Are specific enough to be understood, but not so specific that they feel like there is a solution in the statement
- Are centered on a specific user group (not 'everyone' or 'users')
- Address an actual user need

For example:
- How might we reduce the length of time new customers wait on the phone when calling us?
- How might we help people who have recently lost their job to understand how their skills relate to other jobs?
- How might we help local residents to reduce the amount of waste they need to dispose of?

Bad problem statements:
- How might we encourage people to drive less (describes the solution)
- How might we reduce the amount of material going to waste (too broad, no users)
- How might we get people to return to our website more often (no user need)
- How might we make users visit the website instead of calling the contact centre (includes a solution, no user need)
- How might we use augmented reality to improve warehouse productivity (includes a solution, no user need)

Once you have landed on a problem statement, use that to focus the rest of your planning activities.

WHO WILL ATTEND?

You'll also need to figure out who will attend the workshop.

You want people who have enough knowledge that they'll be able to contribute something to the workshop. Something that I see frequently is that a client wants to run a workshop and involve only very senior people. The problem is, in a lot of cases, those people are too far removed from the day-to-day work to come up with useful ideas. They don't have to be excluded, but make sure you involve people who are actively involved in the topic, to bring a strong lens of reality to the workshop.

You want people who can attend for the entire session. No dropping in and dropping out—this destroys continuity and the group's flow. Every time someone returns, the group has to go back and catch them up. This not only takes time, but it can derail the progress the group has done. If there are people who absolutely should be involved but can't be there for the whole time, plan to have them work together as a small group. That way their absence doesn't disrupt the whole workshop.

It's also important to have diverse thinking styles in the workshop. When everyone has a similar thinking style you will just get outcomes that are similar to the status quo. You want people who are pragmatic and grounded and people who are optimistic. You sometimes need detractors. You need people who have been involved in the topic for a long time and people who are brand new to it. Don't be afraid to mix up personalities as well—involve people who are loud and outspoken, quiet and thoughtful.

Importantly, also make sure you have good, diverse representation of the user group of the problem you are addressing. We all know that a group of educated white guys can't solve problems for people who aren't educated, white or guys. Work hard to genuinely involve a wide range of people who are part of the user group.

Make sure at least some of the people in the workshop will also be carrying the idea forward, not handing it off to someone else to do. A lot of the value in a design thinking workshop is the shared experience and collective decision-making. It doesn't work to have a group come up with the ideas, then hand it off to someone else to implement—all the tacit knowledge and shared experiences are lost.

Also understand job roles, experience and the relative relationships in the group. In particular, learn whether there are very senior and very junior people in the group, and what the culture of the organization is like with respect to hierarchy. In the planning stage you need to know who is there so you can figure out the best way to get people to work together. I cover the actual management of people in Chapter 4.

LOCATION AND VENUE (IN-PERSON WORKSHOPS)

For in-person workshops, you'll need to have a space that the workshop can use for the full time, uninterrupted (and if overnight, able to leave work-in-progress).

Where possible, get away from where people work day-to-day. When people work in their normal location, they can be easily distracted. It's also great to have a change of scene—it's a small thing but people tend to be able to come up with new ideas better when they're in a different environment.

Great workshop rooms have plenty of room to move around, walls or windows that you can use to put up work, and natural light.

It may be tempting to find a location that has breakout rooms, for people to go off and work in small groups. I always choose large single rooms over breakout rooms. You'll have a much more successful workshop if everyone stays and works in one place. Yes, it will be louder. But the energy will be much higher, everyone can see that the rest of the group are getting involved, and it is a much more creative environment. When people go off to breakout rooms (especially if they aren't being observed or facilitated), their energy drops, and they work more slowly.

Make sure you look at the room before the workshop. This will help you figure out how the flow of the workshop is likely to occur and let you prepare supplies (I often need to adapt if the room doesn't have good walls to post work to). If you can't visit, at least get a photo.

If you must use a location that participants use day to day, get in early and change it. Put posters on the wall, move the projector screen to the other end, block out the normal view—anything you can think of to make it feel like a different space.

Also consider whether you'll need an audio-visual system— you may need a projector for slides and instructions and you may need a mic and amplifier for a large room or if you are playing music or video. Check internet access as well if you need it during the workshop.

TECHNOLOGY AND TOOLS (ONLINE WORKSHOPS)

For online workshops, you don't have to find a physical space, but you have just as much to prepare for a technology space.

You'll need a video meeting tool at the very least. If you will be asking people to work in small groups, choose a tool that has breakout rooms (or equivalents—they are called different things in each tool). Also check that it has features like chat, Q&A and an ability to raise hands to interject.

You are likely to tools that allow people to collaborate as well. The main features you will need are a collaborative whiteboard to write on and the ability to create and move around virtual sticky notes. It can be handy to be able to export finished artefacts. If the participants are not in your organization, check the tool's permissions model—it's handy to be able to invite people without them having to sign up.

Make sure you are completely familiar with all the tools, and that you understand not only how to use them but how to invite people and give them access.

TIMING

For workshops that are less than a day, they can be run as a morning session, an afternoon session, or across lunch. All work well, so consider whether there are any goals that would suit a particular structure. For example, if one of the goals is to get the group working well together, it might be good to work either side of a shared lunch. If your participants work 8 hours of normal office hours, avoid evening workshops—everyone is usually too tired to contribute well.

For day-long workshops, plan to run less than six hours of activities—workshops are very tiring and a full eight-hour day is basically impossible.

For multi-day workshops, you might make the days shorter again—perhaps only four or five hours—again, to help people manage energy.

For online workshops, I tend to run quite short sessions (3 hours max), more of them (and extra small activities to catch up between sessions). Staring at a screen is even more tiring than being in person.

If you know that people have school drop-offs, a block of time they must be at work (e.g. checking in first thing in the morning) or other predictable routines, structure the workshop around these activities.

WORKSHOP STRUCTURE AND FLOW

We've talked all about goals and people and location. The other, and probably largest, part of planning is to work out what people will do during the workshop. This is the part I love most—figuring out what kinds of activities to run and how to weave them together seamlessly and in a way that participants can do their best.

Creating a flexible structure

Facilitators all have personal preferences around how much they structure a workshop and how rigorously they enforce it. Some will plan in detail and follow the plan to the letter. Some will start with a rough plan and see where it takes them. I'm somewhere in the middle—I make a fairly detailed plan, but change it if I need to.

The interesting thing about a workshop is that you literally have no idea what's going to happen. Even if you ran the same workshop multiple times, you'd have an entirely different experience each time.

So, you need a *flexible plan*.

If your agenda is too rigid, you'll be frustrated as the workshop doesn't quite run to your plan. If you plan a very linear process, you'll be frustrated as the workshop goes on a tangent, doubles-back on itself (a lot) before moving forward. It's really important to let this happen—otherwise it feels like you're railroading people, which makes them feel like they are not being listened to (because they aren't).

A flexible workshop plan breaks the workshop down into smaller sections, each with their own goals and outcomes. The plan is all about the flow of the workshop, making sure that the outputs from one section are great inputs to the next; and making sure participants have the skills to contribute to each section. A flexible plan also contains some optional sections—in case groups move more quickly than you expect or in case a group is on a roll and you don't want to cut them off mid thought.

In a flexible plan, the total workshop time is broken into proportions, not hours and minutes. This lets you work with the pace of the participants, not to the pace of the clock.

Because I'm often facilitating for groups I've never met, I create more than one plan, and choose one of them once I've met the group and run a warmup activity. By then I'll have a feel for how energetic and active the group will be, and what their background is. It's great to be able to adapt on the fly, but it does take experience to be able to do it.

Activity flow

In most sections of the workshop you will have participants doing some kind of activity, usually in small groups. The only exception to this is if you need to do small presentations towards the beginning (in the context section) to get everyone on the same page.

When considering what you'll have people do in each section, think about:

- How the activities flow together—make sure the outputs of one easily work as into the inputs to the next
- Skills needed for the activity—will people have the skills? Adjust earlier activities to build their skills, or choose an activity that suits the skills they have (see the section on Building skills towards the end of Chapter 3)
- Information people will need to do the activity—where will it come from? Do you need to prepare something, or can an earlier activity give them the information?
- If something unexpected happens, can the activity order be moved around? What would you do if, for example, a fire alarm went off, or lunch turned up half an hour late?
- Short and long versions of each activity—this lets you be flexible with timing but still get the outcomes you need.

- Varied physical modes—sitting and standing; individual and group work; listening and activities.
- Small energizer activities that work well with the workshop topic and don't feel like they are just being done for the sake of an energizer.
- Variety of activity type, so people don't feel like they are doing the same thing over and over.

When you have your activities planned, do a walkthrough of them, simulating the inputs and outputs. Consider all the things that can go wrong and adapt the plan.

But what activities can I run?

At this point you may be expecting me to describe the actual activities in the workshop—to give you some actual warm-up, idea generation and prioritization methods.

The potential activities you can include in a workshop are huge and ever-changing, and this is a deliberately small book about facilitation. Instead of blowing it out with methods, I've included some of my favorite workshop activity resources at the end of the book.

BEFORE THE WORKSHOP

Give participants the best chance to contribute by carefully planning their pre-workshop experience as well.

Pre-workshop homework

There can be value in asking people to do some preparation ahead of the workshop. It can make the context section a lot smoother if people can learn some of what they need ahead.

One reason I do ask people to do homework is an interesting psychological one. When you ask people to consider their thoughts on a topic, and jot them down, they make an internal commitment to them. When they are in a group situation they are more likely to offer those ideas and defend them. This is important if you are worried that a people will be influenced by someone in the group or follow the first idea that is raised.

Preparation work is also good for people who like to reflect, then contribute—workshop activities can otherwise be dominated and controlled by people (like me) who think only as they hear themselves say something.

So, think about whether you need to ask people to do anything before the workshop, and what format the homework takes. Also think about how you can make it as easy as possible for them to do it.

If you do give a preparation task, make sure it can be completed within work hours. Asking people to do it in their personal time disadvantages people with home and caring responsibilities.

Let people know what to expect

As far ahead as you can, send out a rough workshop agenda to help people know what to expect. It doesn't need to be any more detailed than your flexible workshop plan, and perhaps even less detailed.

The reason to provide this is that people may be nervous about what will be expected of them. Make sure they know that they don't have to do any special preparation (unless you have a homework task) and that they don't have to come with special knowledge.

There are pros and cons to giving people the workshop problem statement. The pros are that people will know what the workshop is about and why they are involved. The cons are that they might come armed with too much preparation or fixed ideas about the solution. My preference is to provide just enough information that they know why they are there, but not enough that they can think they've solved the problem, though this is a delicate one to balance.

Also let people know:

- how to find the venue (be very clear about this and include good instruction)
- where to park or how to commute
- what facilities exist (coffee!)
- if there are any special instructions for accessibility
- what the tea/coffee/food arrangements are

And give them your contact details for any last-minute problems.

CHAPTER SUMMARY

To me, planning a design thinking workshop is almost as much fun as facilitating it. It starts with getting a clear understanding of the goals of the workshop, who will be there and where it will be. Then you plan the activities that will form the bulk of the workshop, making sure each builds on the previous and that people will have the skills to do them. And of course, you also have to invite people, explain any homework tasks and clearly explain the flow and logistics for the workshop.

If you've done all that, you're ready to run the actual workshop!

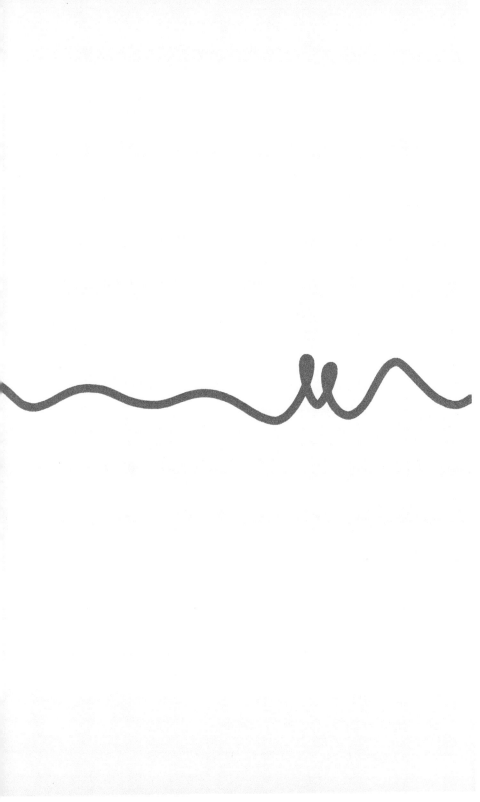

This chapter is all about the how to facilitate the activities and flow of the workshop. Chapter 4 will be about how to look after the people in the workshop.

WORKSHOP INTRODUCTION

The first thing to do in a workshop is to introduce it. This should be quite brief (like, less than 5 minutes). The idea here is to:

- Give people time to physically and mentally settle into the workshop
- Retain the energy they came in with, ready to get started (I'm sure you've sat through a long, boring introduction when you just wanted to get into the fun part)
- Let people know who you are and why you are facilitating
- Let people know your connection to the topic

Introduce yourself with just enough information so people know your name and why you are the person facilitating. The workshop is not about you and a short intro communicates that.

Introduce the topic, again with only enough information for people to know what it's about ("Today we are going to explore the problem of waste in the factory"). You'll talk about the topic endlessly during the workshop so don't need to do it here.

Describe the basic structure of the workshop—a very high level overview. Don't go into detail about everything that will happen during the workshop. Firstly, it will be too much for people to take in, and they don't need to know detail right now. Secondly, if you have a flexible structure, you want to be able to adapt during the workshop if necessary. Mainly explain that it will be about generating ideas and that there will be an opportunity to do this without assessing, judging and critiquing. Explain how the group will work together. And explain how the outcomes will be used.

GREAT WARMUPS

Oh, no! The dreaded icebreaker! We've all been in workshops where the facilitator starts off by saying "let's do an icebreaker" and proceeds to request that you share something personal, play a silly game or something else that feels awkward and a waste of time.

The intent is good. It is necessary to prepare people for the work ahead. It is necessary for them to know who is there and why. And it is necessary for people to start to build trust. It just doesn't need to be as bad as you've likely experienced.

A great warmup gets the group ready for work. It builds people's energy and enthusiasm.

Model the activity structure

Use the warmup to model how activities will run throughout the workshop. For many activities, you'll be providing instruction, participants will work alone or in small groups on an activity, then share back the results and debrief. Do all of these during the warmup as well. It helps people understand how the workshop activities will run and how they will feel.

Match the warmup to the workshop goals

Many warmups feel trivial and disconnected from the workshop. Instead of something that feels trivial, match the warmup activity to the workshop purpose and activities. If you'll later be doing some drawing, make the activity about drawing. If you'll be working on new features for a product, start with an activity related to the current product. If you'll be working with unfamiliar materials (like craft, Lego bricks, or even just sticky notes) the warmup is a chance to use these materials now, so people are more comfortable later.

Don't ask people to reveal personal information

No matter whether a group knows each other or not, people don't like sharing personal information.

I hate when I'm asked to tell two truths and a lie or share something that people don't know about me—the reason they don't know these things about me is that I don't want to share them! I don't know how that information will be used and if it could later be used against me or to make fun of me.

When people are asked to share something personal it is often later used as a 'marker' of that person (e.g. 'the guy who hates chocolate'). It seems funny at first, but very quickly a single thing about you becomes your workshop identity and detracts from the actual skills you bring to the workshop. Don't let this happen.

Make introductions part of the warmup

Make introductions part of the warmup activity—there really is nothing more boring than going around the room with names and job roles. For example, if the warmup activity is to describe and share goals for the workshop, ask participants work silently on that first, then introduce themselves as they share their goals. If the warmup is to do a little drawing, ask them to do that first and introduce themselves as they show their drawing.

Let the group know that they're going to get started straight away and do introductions later, so they don't feel like you've forgotten an important step.

Observe the warmup

In face-to-face workshops, the warmup is a perfect time for you to get an idea of how people work. You'll be able to see who jumps in, who asks their colleague for help, who speaks first, who doesn't seem to want to get involved and how the group works together. This is a great chance to observe and start to adapt the workshop structure and activities. It's harder to do this with an online workshop, though you'll certainly see who starts contributing first, and who jumps in with a question or comment.

INTRODUCING ACTIVITIES

One of your important jobs as a facilitator is to set the scene so the group is ready to start each activity with a clear idea of what to do.

Explain the activity as clearly and succinctly as you can (it should take you less than a minute). Plan this ahead of time and rehearse the instruction. Most people provide an instruction then explain the instruction. That's confusing and hard to follow. Say it once only.

Support the instruction visually

Provide something visual to support your verbal instructions. Keep the instructions visible during the activity. People will often get part way through the activity then need clarification of what they are meant to do—a visual reference gives them the confidence that they are on the right track. This might be a presentation slide or a hand-written instruction stuck to the wall.

This is also handy for people, like me, who just can't process and remember verbal instructions—give us some support and we don't have to embarrass ourselves by asking what you said.

Show an example

If the activity is something that people don't do regularly, show an example of what you want them to do. For example, if you want them to do little thumbnail sketches, show them how to fold paper to make small panels, how to sketch and how fast it is. If you want them to work with craft or Lego bricks, make a small example scene.

One thing at a time

Don't give instruction for more than one activity at a time—let each go through its own cycle. You can explain how the activity will connect to the next one, but don't attempt more than that.

If you have a multi-part activity (where you won't be sharing back and reflecting until the end of all the parts), introduce each part as quickly as you can so the energy of the group doesn't drop. If I have the participants working in small groups I give the instruction to each group one at a time rather than interrupt the whole room.

Communicate time expectations

Participants need to know what size the activity is. Not only does it help them to manage the actual minutes, it also lets them know whether it will feel like a small and fast activity, or a long and reflective one.

Just before they start, tell them what the time will be and how you'll manage it.

Check in

Ask if they're clear about what they should be doing. If you have been very unclear, people will let you know. If they aren't quite sure, they'll usually have a go and then ask.

Let them go

Once you've given an instruction, stand back and let the participants work.

And *stop talking*! I keep seeing facilitators give an instruction, wait for the group to respond, then repeat the instruction, or talk over the top of the group as they start the activity. Give the instruction once, give it clearly then just stop talking.

People will start off relatively slowly—they need to get their head around the activity and figure out who is going to lead the group. They will usually look to the instructions a couple of times to figure out what you asked them to do.

Don't jump in and help! Give people breathing room and let them explore on their own—it's part of the process to deal with uncertainty, and if you support them too soon you'll close down their creativity. If your instructions were actually unclear someone will eventually ask you for clarification.

Keep a casual eye on the activity. Don't stare people down—have something to be doing (preparing the next activity, re-arranging supplies, re-arranging materials on a wall). Observe just closely enough so that you can see if people are very lost, or if they start going completely in the wrong direction.

MANAGING TIME

Another important job as a facilitator is managing the time for an activity.

There are three main ways to manage activity time—tightly time boxed, to a deadline and by observing progress.

One thing I've seen go wrong in design thinking workshops is using time in the wrong way—most often by artificially constraining time for topics that need space.

Time boxing

For a time boxed activity, you set a clearly defined amount of time—usually quite small (5-30 minutes) and stop at the end of the time. Time boxing is great when you need people to just have a go at something—the tight constraint forces people to dive in, potentially loosening up their inhibitions. Time pressure forces people to create work quickly without judging their work. It helps people stay high-level and doesn't give them time to go into too much detail or start critiquing ideas. Let people know that they will feel rushed and that it is deliberate.

If you are going to be keeping time very strictly, use a countdown timer that the whole group can see.

Deadlines

For an activity with a deadline, you'll stop at a memorable point, such as a quarter or half hour, or at a break. Let people know what the deadline is and remind them as they get close to it.

Finish when it's done

The last type is when you observe how the activity is going and wrap it up when people are 'done'. This is good for the most important activities—the ones where you don't want to wrap up too early and miss out on achieving the outcomes. This takes additional facilitation as you have to keep an eye on the groups to track their progress. As you see the groups get through the work, let them know when they have a few minutes left, so they can finish and wrap up.

As the activity progresses, watch the energy of the group. There will usually be a part where they are uncertain and slow to start, and then a very busy middle where they are very much into the work. Then they'll slow down, start to get distracted and do other things. That's when it's good to stop them or move them on to the next part of the activity. Never stop people while they are in the busy middle—as every kid knows it's very frustrating to be in the middle of fun and be told that you have to stop for some artificial reason. It will also disrupt activities that come next, as they'll still be wanting to finish the last piece of their work.

Wrapping up

If the activity is longer than about half an hour, towards the end of the time, check in and let people know how long they have to go—they will not have been paying attention to time. This will give them time to finish the work they're doing and wrap it up.

Have a method prepared for interrupting them so you can give another instruction. Some facilitators use background music and turn the volume down. Some use a special song and turn the volume up. Some use a bell. I'm a master at the quiet librarian shush as music is the thing I most often forget to prepare.

BRAINSTORMING AND IDEA GENERATION

Design thinking workshops will usually have a section (sometimes it's the bulk of the workshop) where the group will come up with ideas related to the workshop topic.

This can be the most challenging part of the workshop— this kind of unbounded idea generation isn't something we do often. If your participants have never done anything like this (and particularly if you know they will take a while to get comfortable working with each other) think about doing a very short round (like, 15 minutes) on a topic unrelated to the workshop, just to show them how it works. This is also handy if the workshop topic has important consequences— you don't want to lose the opportunity to come up with a great outcome just because people don't yet have the right skills for the task.

In the introduction to the idea generation activity, emphasize:

• Getting started is better than being right

- More ideas are always better, even if they seem weird, incorrect or not viable
- There is to be no critiquing of ideas—there are no rights and wrongs at this point

See the resources at the end of the book for ideas for brainstorming and idea generation activities—there are many!

SHARING BACK

For many activities, the group will share their work. They may share to a small group or back to the whole group.

In the introduction to the activity, let them know that this will happen, how it will work and how much time they have. If they need time to prepare a presentation, this can be a mini activity with a whole activity cycle of its own.

Consider asking the group to rotate presenters. The advantage of this is that more people get to contribute and the wider group hears from more perspectives. However, there will be people who are very uncomfortable presenting, and the idea of it may stop them contributing, so don't force it.

Presentation time is one time when, as a facilitator, you need to watch the clock and timekeep precisely. Let one person go over time and everyone will go over time. It is also the place where you can catch up time if you need—reduce the time for each presentation, select a few presentations or have people present to their group instead of everyone presenting to the whole room.

Reflecting

Many activities will have a short reflection. This can be done individually or as a group. It's a chance for people to think about what they just did, what they learned, how it connects to the problem statement as a whole, and how the workshop is progressing overall. It also gives them a moment to stop, breathe and re-centre.

Without a reflection, energy remains at the same level for a long time, which can be very tiring. If possible, run the reflection just before a break.

DOCUMENTING THE ACTIVITY

All activities should have some visual aspect that groups create and share. Documenting the work lets people know that their ideas are being listened to and included. Seeing the work as it evolves shows everyone how the parts of it fit together and gives them concrete representation of their progress.

Many activities are naturally self-documenting. Writing ideas on sticky notes, making structures out of craft, and stories all naturally create their own documentation.

If you are doing a discussion activity, make sure someone is writing it all down. If it's for the whole room, the facilitator can do it. If small groups are working together, assign someone in the group to do it. This also reinforces that contributions are being listened to and valued.

MAKING DECISIONS

There are usually points in a workshop where you need to make decisions as a group. This most often happens when selecting ideas to take forward through the workshop; or selecting ideas to follow up outside of the workshop.

Common ways to do this are with simple voting and prioritization.

Voting

A common voting method, which works reasonably well, is dot voting—here you display the ideas, give people a number of votes (I use 3-5) and get them to vote on the ideas. People can vote by putting actual sticky dots on the idea; or can tick or dot ideas with marker (or equivalent with online tools). I usually let them vote for their own idea and put more than one dot on an idea they love. It's surprising how well this little method works at getting group consensus on what to follow on with.

Prioritisation

A prioritization activity puts the ideas in some kind of order, which helps to choose which one/s to continue to explore. The simplest and most common prioritization method is a 2x2 matrix, where ideas are plotted according to 2 values such as:

- value to customers
- value to the business
- cost
- complexity
- timeframe (now -> later)
- matches the 'how might we' statement

Simply have the participants place out the ideas based on their initial gut feel—you'll be surprised how easy it is to place an idea along a spectrum when they have other ideas to compare to.

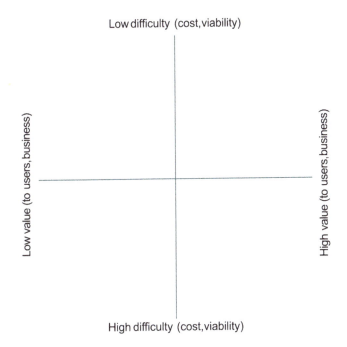

Figure 2: A 2x2 matrix

BUILDING SKILLS

It's important to sequence and run the workshop in a way that, when people get to an activity, they have the skills to do it. Participants don't do these kinds of workshop activities often and may not naturally have experience with the techniques. If you build these skills during the workshop, people will be able to jump into an activity without hesitation.

Sticky notes

Sticky notes are design thinking facilitators' favorite tools. They are useful in all kinds of ways. As the most often used tool, there are some ways to make them work well for you that also makes it easy for participants.

Before any sticky note work, show people how to remove a sticky note sideways from the deck, not upwards (if you've never seen this done—removing it sideways means it will hang straight when stuck on the wall, removing it upwards makes it curl).

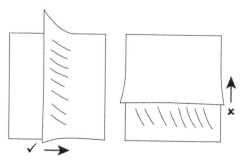

Figure 3: Peel a sticky note from the side, not from bottom to top, and it will sit flat on the wall and not curl up.

Show them how to write a single idea per note, in large writing, with a marker. For online sticky notes, show how much content you want people to write on the note.

Figure 4: Show people how big you expect them to write.

These two things sound trivial, but actually go a long way to helping people feel comfortable—no-one has that awkward moment where they realize they were the only one who wrote an essay on a sticky note!

If you would like to somewhat 'anonymize' who contributed what to a discussion or make sure everyone feels on equal footing, give everyone the same color sticky note and the same color marker. Some people will still stand out because of handwriting, but this lack of differentiation goes a surprisingly long way to democratizing a discussion.

If you would like to be able to see how an activity has built over the workshop, use a different color for each section of the workshop.

If you would like to be able to track the contribution of each group, give each group a different color.

If none of these things matter, let people choose what color sticky note and marker they would like to use.

Sketching

Another method that's common in design thinking workshops is sketching. It's quick, it can be done roughly and used to explore an idea. With fat markers, it encourages people to do just enough to get down an idea and not worry about the details. For designers and facilitators, who sketch a lot, it's a completely natural way of getting ideas down.

However, most people are not comfortable sketching—they just haven't had the practice. If you ask a group to sketch something, a large proportion of them will react with fear and shut down. It's too far out of their comfort zone.

I rarely use the word sketch. Instead, I ask people to doodle, write a story, write a set of dot points, or make something with craft. I am exceptionally careful to make sure that people don't feel like their contribution is less valuable just because it's not a drawing. Because it's not.

If you do really want people to explore and communicate their ideas with drawing, you have to give them the skills. Many workshop facilitators teach basic shapes and basic 'thinking in pictures' to help the group feel comfortable. As long as you have the time to build their skills gradually and practice, this is a good approach. But it can't be done as a token effort at the beginning of a workshop. It really does take time.

Using craft/bricks/things with hands

Many activities, particularly in the idea definition part of a face-to-face workshop, use craft materials or Lego-style bricks.

Facilitators use these kinds of materials because they lower the barrier to entry to an activity. It is easy to pick up some popsicle sticks or Lego bricks and start to make something. People love to fiddle and assemble. Most of us think as we make, which is quite different to having to come up with an idea in your head and then write it down.

For participants, craft activities move the focus to the thing created, not the person who created it. This is very helpful for people who are uncomfortable expressing themselves in a group or worried that the group may judge them. The creation can talk for them. Questions from the group become about the creation, not about the individual.

To help people feel comfortable with craft materials, have them on the table from the beginning of the workshop. Don't mention them, but don't discourage people from using them. As long as there seem to be plenty of materials, people will pick them up and start making things, even while they are waiting for something else to happen. And they'll show off their things to people nearby. This is a fabulous, seemingly accidental, way to get people talking to each other, making things and sharing.

Provide materials that can be assembled and disassembled—this lets people explore and break and not worry that they have come up with the right idea or final solution. For example, don't ask them to glue popsicle sticks together—give them tape or blu tak so they can pull apart and rebuild

as needed. Pencils and erasable pens are good for writing.
Pipe cleaners bend and twist and can be pulled apart.
Provide lots of paper and a place to discard unwanted work.

Working with metaphors

Some design thinking activities have people work with a
metaphor for the problem, rather than tackling the problem
head on. For example, I've been in workshops where we had
to describe our product in terms of an animal, our team in
terms of a vehicle, and an ideal experience by creating a
collage with photographs (not all in the same workshop,
thankfully).

Using a metaphor can help a group think about a problem in
a different way than trying to solve it directly. It can be good
to explore the concepts around the problem as a way to
unpack it. It lets a group discuss sensitive issues without
discussing the actual issue in detail, which is great for
cultures where it us uncommon to discuss sensitive ideas
directly.

The problem can be that many people don't easily think and
work in metaphor. The activity can seem like a silly game as
it doesn't appear to be addressing the issue at hand. They
may then do the activity as if it is a game and not treat it
seriously. I'll admit that I am one of these people—In the
workshops I mentioned above I didn't understand what we
were meant to be doing and contributed something flippant
and silly. Imagine my surprise when that silly, flippant answer
ended up being considered as if it was real, and made it to
the end result! Oops!

Another disadvantage is that using metaphor allows people
to use stereotypes and shortcuts to represent concepts. For
example, asking what animal represents your product leads
to a lot of answers that represent stereotypical features of
animals. Stereotyping can introduce significant bias and stop
people from thinking about the actual consequence of what
they are discussing.

If you think that a metaphor activity is a good way to achieve a goal (don't get me wrong, it can be):

- Explain the activity clearly
- Explain how you will use the outcome of it
- Give people a way to do an alternate version if they would like to address the topic head-on

WRAPPING UP THE WORKSHOP

The end of the workshop may seem like a time where you can finally stop facilitating everything and just let it happen.

Not so! To give people closure from what is often a quite intense experience, be as careful about this as the rest of the workshop.

Plan to finish the workshop a bit earlier than scheduled—people are always pleasantly surprised when they get an 'early mark'.

Summarize the workshop progress—show how far the group got in a very short time. If you did an activity at the beginning around workshop expectations, reflect on whether those expectations were met (and if they aren't, which often happens, why not and what happened instead). Thank everyone. Reiterate how valuable their contribution was. Remind them of what happens next.

Take some time packing up or hang around on the call—you'll be surprised who shares additional ideas or asks questions they didn't want to ask during the workshop. These little interactions are sometimes very important. I've often wondered why a group is behaving in a particular way right throughout the workshop, and someone only tells me at the very end…

CHAPTER SUMMARY

Running the workshop is so much fun. If it goes well, it's loud and active and creative. You'll be juggling a lot as it runs (but your planning will have prepared you for it). Your main jobs will be to briefly introduce yourself and the topic, introduce the activities, keep time and manage the flow of each activity. There's a lot to do.

In this chapter I covered the mechanics of the activities. In the next you'll learn about the final, and hardest part— managing the people!

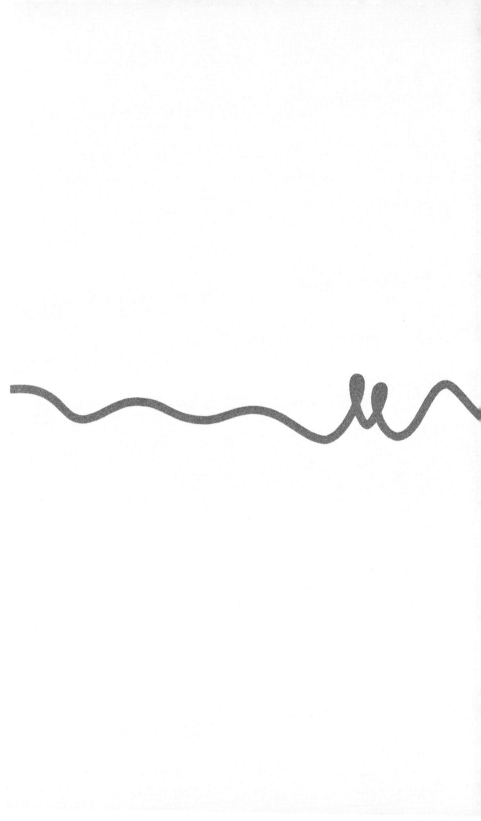

Finally, the most fun part of facilitating a design thinking workshop—looking after the people in the room.

This is also the hardest part to learn as it's very much based on experiencing all of the things that happen when you ask people to work together. But I can at least give you some techniques and tips.

MAKING SURE EVERYONE CONTRIBUTES

One of the main values of design thinking workshops over regular meetings is that they are truly collaborative and use the experience of everyone in the group. That means that everyone needs to participate.

Groups are complex things, and groups with existing work patterns and hierarchies are particularly complex. You will need to take very deliberate steps to make sure everyone can and does contribute. Don't just hope it will work out—it may not.

Thinking then contributing

One approach is to give people time to work on their own, then come together and discuss. They might do an individual brainstorm on sticky notes, some individual sketching or write some stories.

The value of this is:

- people who prefer to think then talk are given time to contribute (these people are used to being talked over)
- people who usually talk first still get to contribute but must give space to others
- topics that require thought and reflection are given the time and attention they need
- the group doesn't latch onto the first idea said out loud
- the number and range of ideas are larger than if the group just started talking

After they have had time to work alone, everyone shares what they came up with. When people are sharing back, keep an eye out to see if anyone throws away or hides their work—sometimes people are reluctant to contribute after they've heard other ideas (don't necessarily force them to add their ideas, but observe the behavior and think about what you might need to do about it).

Turn taking

Another way to make sure everyone contributes is to force turn taking. As a facilitator you tell the group what the sequence is, and people take turns in that sequence.

Vary the turn-taking so the same people don't always go first. You can change the direction, start in different places in the group, get every second person to contribute. You can also limit the amount that people contribute each turn—maybe everyone adds 2 sticky notes from a brainstorming activity, not their whole list.

This is an especially good way of helping a mixed hierarchy group work together. At least for the first few rounds, make sure the highest-ranked people go last.

MANAGING GROUPS

Forming groups

Almost all design thinking workshops will break off into small groups at some point. You have many options around how to form groups, and it depends on the goal of the workshop and the culture of the group:

Let people form their own groups. When people self-select they will probably work well together. However, they might miss out on creative ideas if they fall into existing work patterns. You'll also need to step in to make sure everyone is part of a group.

Use mixed-hierarchy or mixed-role groups. This is good if part of the goal is for people to get an understanding of the experience of people they don't interact with often.

Use same-hierarchy or same-role groups. These groups usually work together easily. The workshop as a whole will often have a bigger diversity of ideas as each group focuses on their experience or perspective.

When planning the activities for the workshop, consider what the groups will do. Will you ask them to all do the same activity and report back? Or will they do different activities related to their expertise?

Getting people working together

No matter whether people do or don't know each other, it's hard to get started with group work. The group has to understand what they are meant to do, figure out who's going to be the leader, who's going to be the decision-maker and who are the do-ers (and no, these aren't assigned roles—these are natural roles that happen in groups).

To get groups working well together:

- Use the warmup to start the process. A non-threatening warmup activity helps the group get over the initial barriers to working together.
- Start with small, well-defined activities—don't make your first activity an hour long, with many steps and difficult work. Build up to more challenging activities gradually.
- In early activities, assign deliberate roles—for example, tell the group to choose a note-taker, a tie-breaker (a person who helps make decisions when the group is stuck) and a reporter.

Getting groups unstuck

Sometimes a group will hit a wall. They'll be working through an activity and will just feel unable to make progress. See if you can analyze what's happening, as that will give you clues as to how to solve it:

Are they lost in the instruction? You might just need to clarify the instruction and get them back on track.

Did they follow a tangent that now doesn't work for the activity? Get them to backtrack, see where they went down the current path and redirect them.

Is one group member causing the group to close off? See if you can figure out what their behavior is. Perhaps give people solo tasks for a short period and bring them back together to summarize—this can help if an individual is trying to direct the activity.

Are their skills sufficient? Consider what you asked them to do and if they actually have the skills to do it. Offer them an alternative way to get to the same goal with the skills they have.

Feeling safe in the group

People need to feel safe before contributing to a group and sharing their work.

Sometimes you'll have a group of people who already know each other; that you thought would work well together but are just not working well. You'll never know for sure, but it is possible that their existing relationship is getting in the way. People might be afraid that what they do in the workshop will have repercussions later, or they may have experiences with a group member that means they aren't able to contribute.

You'll never get people to start trusting each other if trust has already been broken, so there is no tip or trick for making that happen. If it's possible to isolate it, see if you can re-structure groups. Or break the activity into smaller groups with more solo activities and sharing back than collaborative work.

Not feeling stupid

People hate feeling stupid in front of others. You might see people throwing away work, doing work then not sharing it, or not doing the work at all.

Managing this is similar to other group management tips:
- Make activities smaller rather than larger, so people feel like they can attempt the activity
- Provide very clear instructions
- Continually assess whether people's skills are sufficient for the activity, and downgrade it if needed
- Model good behavior when groups share their ideas, so people know they won't be judged or laughed at
- Don't make them go first in sharing work
- Let them hide in the group a little rather than make them uncomfortable

ELEPHANTS IN THE ROOM

Have you ever been in a workshop where everyone knows about something important, or a constraint that will cause problems, but are not talking about it? That's an elephant in the room. These elephants trample on many of our workshops and if you're an external facilitator they may be hard to spot.

To identify elephants:
- In the planning stages, ask your client whether there are any
- If you do an activity that sets the current context, try to spot the elephant there

- If you're thinking there is one, take someone aside and see if they'll explain it

Once you know about the elephant there are many options:

- Do an activity that is about describing it and its consequences (this is only possible if the elephant is not literally in the room—sometimes the 'elephant' is someone senior and the way they behave).
- Acknowledge that it exists and that you can't do anything about it now.
- Decide whether your activities should reflect the current elephant-filled scenario; or whether they should reflect a more idealistic scenario.
- Leave the elephant alone but understand how it is affecting what people are coming up with.

PET PROJECTS

People will come into the workshop with all of their own opinions, background and agendas. One of the reasons we run activities in design thinking workshops is to help participants focus on working on a problem together and not just on talking through the same issues that they've been talking about for a long time.

As groups work through activities, keep an eye and ear out to see if anyone is drifting from the topic at hand and into their own agenda or pet project. You will usually spot it in two situations:

- When they have more time than they need and have finished the core of the activity
- When presenting their work

In the first case, you can wrap up the activity or give them some extra work to do. In the second, as soon as they stop presenting the work and start presenting their thoughts, just wrap them up, or ask how their comment relates to the activity they just completed.

WHEN PEOPLE SAY OR DO ODD THINGS

The hardest things to plan for are all the unusual things that people may say or do. We can plan a flexible structure, have back-up activities and know that there will be some difficulties getting people to work. What we can't prepare for are the things that people say or do that surprise us. Luckily it does get easier with practice.

Some of the 'odd' things I've seen and had to react to have included:

- Racism, sexism and a very wide range of disdainful and disrespectful comments
- Interruptions that have nothing to do with the topic
- Getting up and walking out of the room
- Interfering with the completed work of another group
- Outright hostility towards the workshop or an activity

I generally try to:
- Not react surprised or shocked. This comes with experience and over time you'll be able to straight-face just about anything.
- Give the person a moment—the unexpected thing may seem unusual at the beginning and then resolve without intervention, or one of the group may intervene.
- Reiterate the question/instruction for the activity in case they've misunderstood and gone in an unexpected direction. Ask questions to help draw out how they see it as being relevant to the topic under discussion.
- Potentially just ignore it and don't give it any attention (if it seems like the behavior is attention-seeking).

However, it is also your job to protect the group. You must gently, or even strongly, redirect anything offensive or harassing.

CHAPTER SUMMARY

Managing people is hard but is very rewarding when you see people work well together and produce great results. In the planning stages you consider how you will get people to work together. In the room you think on your feet, observe, analyze and support people as they make their way through the workshop. You also will be listening out for, and getting ready for odd things, like elephants that seem to trample the work, people's pet projects and odd things that people say and do. You'll get better at this skill every single time you stand in front of a group.

Honestly, that's almost everything you need to know to run a great design thinking workshop. Just a couple of last tips about online workshops...

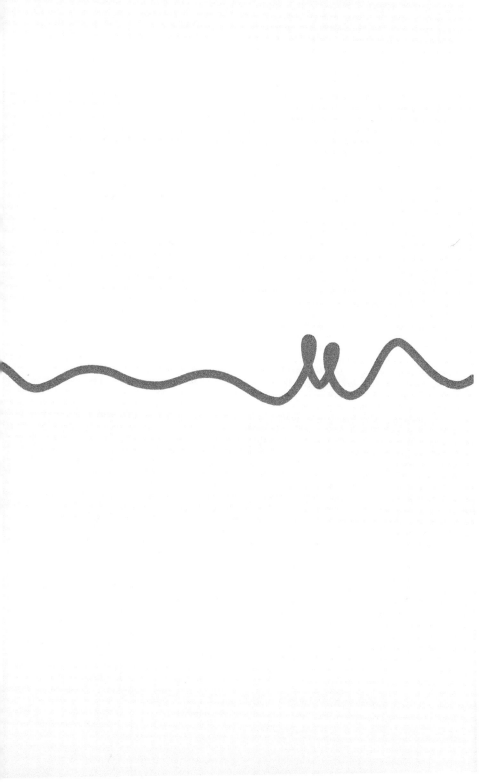

Almost all the principles in previous chapters apply to face to face and online in pretty much the same way. All the workshop planning is the same in principle and managing the workshop itself is fairly similar.

However, there are a few specifics you might consider for an online workshop.

ALL IN-PERSON OR ALL ONLINE

Don't blend online and face to face groups. If you're doing an online workshop, have everyone online. If you attempt to blend them, your timing and pacing won't work, you'll have to give two sets of instructions, and reporting back will be difficult.

PACE

Online workshops are slower than face to face workshops—it takes longer for people to figure out how to work together, it takes longer to wrap up activities and bring the group back together (or to get people to return after breaks) and it takes longer to, for example create a sticky note in a whiteboarding tool and find it again than doing it with paper and a marker. If you're accustomed to in-person workshops, add about 20% extra time.

TECHNOLOGY SKILLS

Participants not only have to learn workshop skills, they have to learn technology skills. Plan a way to help them learn these skills—you might do a half-hour technology-familiarization meeting ahead of the workshop (a few days ahead so people can then play with any tools you'll be using) or you might just add time at the beginning of each activity to discuss and practice how to use the tool.

GROUP SIZE

I usually manage groups a bit differently. In a face-to-face workshop, I'll usually have people work in groups of 5-6. For an online workshop, smaller groups can work well. Consider the group dynamic though—teams who already work together online may be good in larger groups, but people who don't know each other are likely better in smaller groups.

ATTENTION

It's easier for people to be distracted and 'check out' of the activities. Structure your activities to make sure everyone has a chance to contribute and reinforce that they will be expected to contribute and share.

CHAPTER SUMMARY

Most of the principles in the book apply equally to in-person and online workshops. The main differences with online workshops are that their pace is often slower, people need to learn the technology, you may make groups smaller, and you'll need to take steps to make sure people are present and contributing.

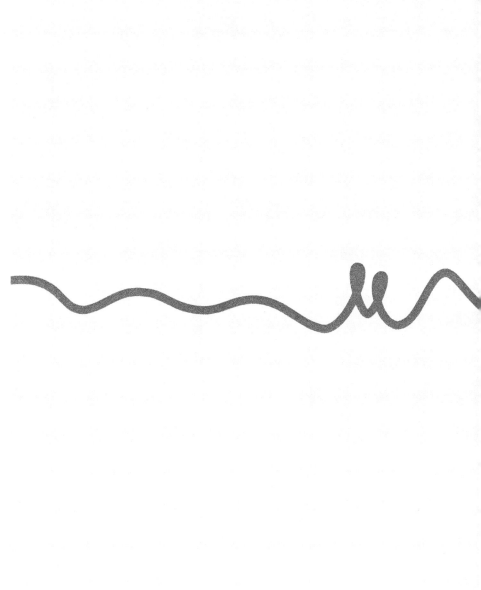

Design thinking workshops are a great way to get a group of people together to work on a problem, get a shared understanding and come up with creative solutions.

But they don't happen without deliberate work—planning the workshop, structuring the activities and then facilitating the workshop itself. They also take experience in working with people, which takes time to learn.

In this short book, I've used my experience to outline what goes into planning and facilitating a great workshop. I hope that in your next workshop, your participants feel energized, able to contribute and valued. I hope they see a useful outcome from their time and effort and are keen to get involved further. And I hope that you feel confident and keen to run more workshops and continue learning.

RESOURCES

Design thinking in general

Article. *What is Design Thinking and Why Is It So Popular?* Rikke Friis Dam and Teo Yu Siang, Interaction Design Foundation. https://www.interaction-design.org/literature/article/what-is-design-thinking-and-why-is-it-so-popular

Article. *5 Stages in the Design Thinking Process.* Rikke Friis Dam and Teo Yu Siang, Interaction Design Foundation. https://www.interaction-design.org/literature/article/5-stages-in-the-design-thinking-process

Article. *Why Design Thinking Works.*, Harvard Business Review https://hbr.org/2018/09/why-design-thinking-works

Online workshops

Article. *The Remote Design Sprint Guide.* Jake Knapp, John Zeratsky, Jackie Colburn, Sprint. https://www.thesprintbook.com/remote

Workshop methods

Book. *Gamestorming: A Playbook for Innovators, Rulebreakers, and Changemakers.* Dave Gray, Sunni Brown and James Macanufo. 1st edition, 2010

Book. *50 Remote-Friendly Icebreakers.* Ben Crothers. https://remotefriendlyicebreakers.com/

Website. *Gamestorming website:* https://gamestorming.com/

Facilitation

Book. *Building a Better Business Using the Lego Serious Play Method.* Per Kristiansen, Robert Rasmussen. 1st edition, 2014

Book. *Unlocking the Magic of Facilitation: 11 Key Concepts You Didn't Know You Didn't Know.* Killermann, Sam; Bolger, Meg. Impetus Books. 1st edition, 2016.

Book. *Work the Room: Leading collaboration in wonderful workshops.* Austin Govella. 1st edition, 2023.

INDEX

A

activities 25
activities, introducing 32

B

brainstorming and idea
generation 36

D

decisions 38
  prioritisation 39
  voting 39
design thinking
  examples 3
  what is 3
design thinking workshops
  a real example 9
  general approach 6
  good for 6, 15
  not good for 15
  participants 6

F

facilitator's role 13
flexible structure 23

H

how might we 17

L

location / venue 20

M

metaphors 44

O

online workshops 56

P

participants 19
problem statements 17

S

sketching 42
sticky notes 40

T

time
  time boxing 34
  managing 34

W

warmups 30
workshop goals 13

ABOUT THE AUTHOR

Donna Spencer is a product designer. She has extensive experience in user experience, service design, workshop facilitation and information architecture. She has worked in government, education, with startups and much more.

She is a regular conference and meetup speaker, article author and has written 5 UX-related books (including this one!). She was the founder of UX Australia and ran it for 9 years. She sews, weaves and knits, and is currently renovating an old house. Her cats are known around the world as they like to 'contribute' to all presentations and meetings.